Ron on the Run

by Alice Cary
illustrated by Olivia Cole

Practice Decodable 26

McGraw Hill Education

Bothell, WA • Chicago, IL • Columbus, OH • New York, NY

MHEonline.com

Send all inquiries to:
McGraw-Hill Education
8787 Orion Place
Columbus, OH 43240

ISBN: 978-0-02-145635-2
MHID: 0-02-145635-6

Printed in the United States of America.

7 8 9 CTM 23

The sun is up.
Ron is on the run.

Ron dusts and mops.

Ron has a cup and a bun.

A dump truck hits mud.
Mud hits Ron.

The bus hits mud.

Ron sits in muck.

If Ron sits in muck, Ron can get sad.